OFFICE *of* INVESTOR
EDUCATION *and* ADVOCACY

Before You Invest, **Investor.gov**

MUTUAL FUNDS and ETFS

A Guide for Investors

Mutual Funds and Exchange-Traded Funds (ETFs)

American investors often turn to mutual funds and exchange-traded funds (ETFs) to save for retirement and other financial goals. Although mutual funds and ETFs have similarities, they have differences that may make one option preferable for any particular investor. This brochure explains the basics of mutual fund and ETF investing, how each investment option works, the potential costs associated with each option, and how to research a particular investment.

U.S. Securities and Exchange Commission
Office of Investor Education and Advocacy
100 F Street, NE
Washington, DC 20549-0213
Toll-free: (800) 732-0330
Website: www.Investor.gov

Table of Contents

Key Points to Remember

- Mutual funds and ETFs are not guaranteed or insured by the FDIC or any other government agency—even if you buy through a bank and the fund carries the bank's name. You can lose money investing in mutual funds or ETFs.

- Past performance is not a reliable indicator of future performance, so don't be dazzled by last year's high returns. But past performance can help you assess a fund's volatility over time.

- All mutual funds and ETFs have costs that lower your investment returns. Shop around and compare fees.

How Mutual Funds and ETFs Work

How Mutual Funds Work

A mutual fund is an SEC-registered open-end investment company that pools money from many investors and invests the money in stocks, bonds, short-term money-market instruments, other securities or assets, or some combination of these investments. The combined securities and assets the mutual fund owns are known as its portfolio, which is managed by an SEC-registered investment adviser. Each mutual fund share represents an investor's proportionate ownership of the mutual fund's portfolio and the income the portfolio generates.

Investors in mutual funds buy their shares from, and sell/redeem their shares to, the mutual funds themselves. Mutual fund shares are typically purchased from the fund directly or through investment professionals like brokers. Mutual funds are required by law to price their shares each business day and they typically do so after the major U.S. exchanges close. This price—the per-share value of the mutual fund's assets minus its liabilities—is called the NAV or net asset value. Mutual funds must sell and redeem their shares at the NAV that is calculated after the investor places a purchase or redemption order. This means that, when an investor places a purchase order for mutual fund shares during the day, the investor won't know what the purchase price is until the next NAV is calculated.

Types of Investment Companies

There are three basic types of investment companies:

Open-end investment companies or ***open-end funds***—which sell shares on a continuous basis, purchased from, and redeemed by, the fund (or through a broker for the fund);

Closed-end investment companies or ***closed-end funds***—which sell a fixed number of shares at one time (in an initial public offering) that later trade on a secondary market; and

Unit Investment Trusts (UITs)—which make a one-time public offering of only a specific, fixed number of redeemable securities called units and which will terminate and dissolve on a date that is specified at the time the UIT is created.

Mutual funds are open-end funds. ETFs are generally structured as open-end funds, but can also be structured as UITs. ETFs operate pursuant to SEC exemptive orders.

How ETFs Work

Like mutual funds, ETFs are SEC-registered investment companies that offer investors a way to pool their money in a fund that makes investments in stocks, bonds, other assets or some combination of these investments and, in return, to receive an interest in that investment pool. Unlike mutual funds, however, ETFs do not sell individual shares directly to, or redeem their individual shares directly from, retail investors. Instead, ETF shares are traded throughout the day on national stock exchanges and at market prices that may or may not be the same as the NAV of the shares.

ETF sponsors enter into contractual relationships with one or more Authorized Participants—financial institutions which are typically large broker-dealers. Typically, only Authorized Participants purchase and redeem shares directly from the ETF. In addition, they can do so only in large blocks (e.g., 50,000 ETF shares) commonly called creation units, and they typically "pay" for the creation units in an in-kind exchange with a group or basket of securities and other assets that generally mirrors the ETF's portfolio.

Once an Authorized Participant receives the block of ETF shares, the Authorized Participant may sell the ETF shares in the secondary market to investors. An ETF share is trading at a premium when its market price is higher than the value of its underlying holdings. An ETF share is trading at a discount when its market price is lower than the value of its underlying holdings. A history of the end-of-day premiums and discounts that an ETF experiences—i.e., its NAV per share compared to its closing market price per share—can usually be found on the website of the ETF or its sponsor. Like a mutual fund, an ETF must calculate its NAV at least once every day.

A Word about *Exchange-Traded Products (ETPs)*

ETFs are just one type of investment within a broader category of financial products called exchange-traded products (ETPs). ETPs constitute a diverse class of financial products that seek to provide investors with exposure to financial instruments, financial benchmarks, or investment strategies across a wide range of asset classes. ETP trading occurs on national securities exchanges and other secondary markets, making ETPs widely available to market participants including individual investors.

Other types of ETPs include exchange-traded commodity funds and exchange-traded notes (ETNs). Exchange-traded commodity funds are structured as trusts or partnerships that physically hold a precious metal or that hold a portfolio of futures or other derivatives contracts on certain commodities or currencies. ETNs are secured debt obligations of financial institutions that trade on a securities exchange. ETN payment terms are linked to the performance of a reference index or benchmark, representing the ETN's investment objective. ETNs are complex, involve many risks for interested investors, and can result in the loss of the entire investment.

This brochure discusses only ETFs that are registered as open-end investment companies or unit investment trusts under the Investment Company Act of 1940. It does not address other types of ETPs, such as exchange-traded commodity funds or ETNs.

Common Features of Mutual Funds and ETFs

Some common features of mutual funds and ETFs are described below. Whether any particular feature is an advantage or disadvantage for you will depend on your unique circumstances—always be sure that the investment you are considering has the features that are important to you.

■ **Professional Management.** Most funds and ETFs are managed by investment advisers who are registered with the SEC.

■ **Diversification.** Spreading investments across a wide range of companies or industry sectors can help lower risk if a company or sector fails. Many investors find it less expensive to achieve such diversification through ownership of certain mutual funds or certain ETFs than through ownership of individual stocks or bonds.

■ **Low Minimum Investment.** Some mutual funds accommodate investors who don't have a lot of money to invest by setting relatively low dollar amounts for the initial purchase, subsequent monthly purchases, or both. Similarly, ETF shares can often be purchased on the market for relatively low dollar amounts.

■ **Liquidity and Trading Convenience.** Mutual fund investors can readily redeem their shares at the next calculated NAV—minus any fees and charges assessed on redemption—on any business day. Mutual funds must send investors payment for the shares within seven days, but many funds provide payment sooner. ETF investors can trade their shares on the market at any time the market is open at the market price—minus any fees and charges incurred at the time of sale. ETF and mutual fund shares traded through a broker are required to settle in three business days.

■ **Costs Despite Negative Returns.** Investors in mutual funds must pay sales charges, annual fees, management fees and other expenses (discussed on pages 27-36), regardless of how the mutual fund performs. Investors may also have to pay taxes on any capital gains distribution they receive. Investors in ETFs must pay brokerage commissions, annual fees, management fees and other expenses (discussed on pages 27-36), regardless of how the ETF performs. ETF investors may also have to pay taxes on any capital gains distributions; however, because of the structure of certain ETFs that redeem proceeds in kind, taxes on ETF investments have historically been lower than those for mutual fund investments. It is important to note that the tax efficiency of ETFs is not relevant if an investor holds the mutual fund or ETF investment in a tax-advantaged account, such as an IRA or a 401(k).

■ **Lack of Control.** Investors in both mutual funds and ETFs cannot directly influence which securities are included in the funds' portfolios.

■ **Potential Price Uncertainty.** With an individual stock or an ETF, an investor can obtain real-time (or close to real-time) pricing information with relative ease by checking financial websites or by calling a broker. By contrast, with a mutual fund, the price at which an investor purchases or redeems shares will depend on the fund's NAV, which the fund might not calculate until many hours after an order has been placed.

Factors to Consider

Before Investing in Mutual Funds or ETFs:

■ **Determine your financial goals and risk tolerance.**
When it comes to investing in mutual funds and ETFs,
investors have thousands of choices. Before you invest
in any mutual fund or ETF, you must decide whether the
investment strategy and risks are a good fit for you. You
should also consider more generally whether the unique
style of investing of the mutual fund's or ETF's sponsor is
a good fit for you. The first step to successful investing is
to figure out your current financial goals and risk tolerance—either on your own or with the help of an investment professional.

■ **Beware of risk.** All investments carry some level of
risk. An investor can lose some or all of the money he or
she invests—the principal—because securities held by a
fund go up and down in value. Dividend payments may
also fluctuate as market conditions change. Mutual funds
and ETFs have different risks and rewards. Generally, the
higher the potential return, the higher the risk of loss.

■ **Consider the sponsor's investing style.** Before you invest, you may want to research the sponsor of the mutual
fund or ETF you are considering. The sponsor's website
is often a good place to begin, and it is helpful to spend

some time browsing through the website to get a better understanding of the sponsor's underlying philosophy on investing. Each sponsor has its own style of investing that will affect how it manages its mutual funds and ETFs. It is helpful to understand each sponsor's style of investing, so you can better choose the right investment for you.

▪ **Ask and check.** Before you engage an investment professional or purchase shares of a mutual fund or ETF, make sure you research and verify relevant information to determine which option is best suited for you.

- Investment professionals: Details on an investment professional's background and qualifications are available on the SEC's Investment Adviser Public Disclosure (IAPD) website (www.adviserinfo.sec.gov/) or on the SEC's website for individual investors, Investor.gov. If you have any questions about checking the background of an investment professional, you can call the SEC's toll-free investor assistance line at (800) 732-0330 for help.

- Mutual funds and ETFs: You can research a mutual fund or ETF by reading its prospectus (discussed on pages 41-43) carefully to learn about its investment strategy and the potential risks. You can find the prospectus on the mutual fund's or ETF's website or on the SEC's EDGAR database (www.sec.gov/ edgar/searchedgar/mutualsearch.html) and download the documents for free.

A Word about *Derivatives*

Derivatives are financial instruments whose performance is derived, at least in part, from the performance of an underlying asset, security, or index. Even small market movements can dramatically affect their value, sometimes in unpredictable ways.

There are many types of derivatives with many different uses. A mutual fund's or ETF's prospectus will disclose whether and how it may use derivatives. An investor may also want to call a fund and ask how it uses these instruments.

Different Types of Mutual Funds And ETFs

Mutual funds and ETFs fall into several main categories. Some are bond funds (also called fixed income funds), and some are stock funds (also called equity funds). There are also funds that invest in a combination of these categories, such as balanced funds and target date funds, and newer types of funds such as alternative funds, smart-beta funds and esoteric ETFs. In addition, there are money market funds, which are a specific type of mutual fund.

■ Bond Funds

Bond funds invest primarily in bonds or other types of debt securities. They generally have higher risks than money market funds (discussed on pages 20-21), largely because they typically pursue strategies aimed at producing higher yields. Unlike money market funds, the SEC's rules do not restrict bond funds to high-quality or short-term investments. Because there are many different types of bonds, bond funds can vary dramatically in their risks and rewards.

Some of the risks associated with bond funds include:

- Credit Risk—the possibility that companies or other issuers whose bonds are owned by the fund may fail to pay their debts (including the debt owed to holders of their bonds). Credit risk is less of a factor for bond funds that invest in insured bonds or U.S. Treasury Bonds. By contrast, those that invest in the bonds of companies with poor credit ratings generally will be subject to higher risk;

- Interest Rate Risk—the risk that the market value of the bonds will go down when interest rates go up. Because of this, an investor can lose money in any bond fund, including those that invest only in insured bonds or U.S. Treasury Bonds. Funds that invest in longer-term bonds tend to have higher interest rate risk; and,

• Prepayment Risk—the chance that a bond will be paid off early. For example, if interest rates fall, a bond issuer may decide to pay off (or retire) its debt and issue new bonds that pay a lower rate. When this happens, the fund may not be able to reinvest the proceeds in an investment with as high a return or yield.

▥ Stock Funds

Stock funds invest primarily in stocks, which are also known as equities. Although a stock fund's value can rise and fall quickly (and dramatically) over the short term, historically, stocks have performed better over the long term than other types of investments—including corporate bonds, government bonds, and treasury securities.

Stock funds can be subject to various investment risks, including **Market Risk**, which poses the greatest potential danger for investors in stock funds. Stock prices can fluctuate for a broad range of reasons—such as the overall strength of the economy or demand for particular products or services.

▥ Balanced Funds

Balanced funds invest in stocks and bonds and sometimes money market instruments in an attempt to reduce risk but still provide capital appreciation and income. They are also known as asset allocation funds and typically hold a relatively fixed allocation of the categories of portfolio instruments. But the allocation will differ from balanced fund to balanced fund. These funds are designed to reduce risk by diversifying among investment categories, but they still share the same risks that are associated with the underlying types of instruments.

◾ Target Date Funds

Also called target date retirement funds or lifecycle funds, these funds also invest in stocks, bonds, and other investments. Target date funds are designed to be long-term investments for individuals with particular retirement dates in mind. The name of the fund often refers to its target retirement date or target date. For example, there are funds with names such as "Portfolio 2050," "Retirement Fund 2050," or "Target 2050" that are designed for individuals who intend to retire in or near the year 2050. Most target date funds are designed so that the fund's allocation of investments will automatically change over time in a way that is intended to become more conservative as the target date approaches. That means that funds typically shift over time from a mix with a lot of stock investments in the beginning to a mix weighted more toward bonds.

Even if they share the same target date, target date funds may have very different investment strategies and risks and the timing of their allocation changes may be different. They also may have different investment results and may charge different fees. Often a target date fund invests in other funds, and fees may be charged by both the target date fund and the other funds. In addition, target date funds do not guarantee that an investor will have sufficient retirement income at the target date, and investors can lose money. Target date funds are generally associated with the same risks as the underlying investments.

▩ Alternative Funds

Alternative funds are funds that invest in alternative investments such as non-traditional asset classes (e.g., global real estate or currencies) and illiquid assets (e.g., private debt) and/or employ non-traditional trading strategies (e.g., selling short). They are sometimes called "hedge funds for the masses" because they are a way to get hedge fund-like exposure in a registered fund. These funds generally seek to produce positive returns that are not closely correlated to traditional investments or benchmarks. Many investors may see alternative funds as a way to diversify their portfolios while retaining liquidity. The risks associated with these investments vary depending on the assets and trading strategies employed. These funds can employ complicated investment strategies, and their fees and expenses are commonly higher than traditionally managed funds. In addition, these types of funds generally have limited performance histories, and it is unclear how they will perform in periods of market stress.

▪ Smart-Beta Funds

These funds are index funds (discussed below) with a twist. They compose their index by ranking stock using preset factors relating to risk and return, such as growth or value, and not simply by market capitalization as most traditional index funds do. They aim to achieve better returns than traditional index funds, but at a lower cost than active funds. These funds can be more complicated and have higher expenses than traditional index funds, and the factors are sometimes based on hypothetical, backward-looking returns. In addition, these types of funds generally have limited performance histories, and it is unclear how they will perform in periods of market stress.

▪ Esoteric ETFs

Esoteric or exotic funds are ETFs that focus on niche investments or narrowly focused strategies. They may be complicated investments and may have higher expenses. In addition, these ETFs are often thinly traded, which means they can be harder to sell and may have larger bid-ask spreads (discussed on page 32) than ETFs that aren't as thinly traded.

A Word about *Hedge Funds*

Hedge fund is a general, non-legal term used to describe private, unregistered investment pools that traditionally have been limited to sophisticated, wealthy investors. Hedge funds are *not* mutual funds and, as such, are *not* subject to the numerous regulations that apply to mutual funds for the protection of investors—including regulations requiring that mutual fund shares be redeemable at any time, regulations protecting against conflicts of interest, regulations to assure fairness in the pricing of fund shares, disclosure regulations, regulations limiting the use of leverage, and more.

▩ Money Market Funds

Money market funds are a type of mutual fund that has relatively low risks compared to other mutual funds and ETFs (and most other investments). By law, they can invest in only certain high-quality, short-term investments issued by the U.S. Government, U.S. corporations, and state and local governments. Government and retail money market funds try to keep their NAV at a stable $1.00 per share, but the NAV may fall below $1.00 if the fund's investments perform poorly. Investor losses have been rare, but they are possible.

- A *Government Money Market Fund* is a money market fund that invests 99.5% or more of its total assets in cash, government securities and/or repurchase

agreements that are collateralized solely by government securities or cash.

- A *Retail Money Market Fund* is a money market fund
that has policies and procedures reasonably designed to limit all beneficial owners of the money
market fund to natural persons.

Other money market funds, however, have a floating
NAV like other mutual funds that fluctuates along with
changes in the market-based value of their portfolio
securities.

All money market funds pay dividends that generally reflect short-term interest rates, and historically the
returns for money market funds have been lower than
for either bond or stock funds. A risk commonly associated with money market funds is **Inflation Risk**, which is
the risk that inflation will outpace and erode investment
returns over time.

Different Types of Investment Strategies

Index-based Funds

Index-based mutual funds and ETFs seek to track an
underlying securities index and achieve returns that
closely correspond to the returns of that index with
low fees. They generally invest primarily in the compo-
nent securities of the index and typically have lower
management fees than actively managed funds. Some
index funds may also use derivatives (such as options

or futures) to help achieve their investment objective. Index-based funds with seemingly similar benchmarks can actually be quite different and can deliver very different returns. For example, some index funds invest in all of the companies included in an index; other index funds invest in a representative sample of the companies included in an index. Because an index fund tracks the securities on a particular index, it may have less flexibility than a non-index fund to react to price declines in the securities contained in the index. Also because market indexes themselves have no expenses, even a passively managed index fund can underperform its index due to fees and taxes.

■ Actively Managed Funds

The adviser of an actively managed mutual fund or ETF may buy or sell components in the portfolio on a daily basis without regard to conformity with an index, provided that the trades are consistent with the overall investment objective of the fund. Unlike similar mutual funds, actively managed ETFs are required to publish their holdings daily. Because there is no underlying index that can serve as a point of reference for investors and other market participants as to the ETF's holdings, disclosing the specific fund holdings ensures that market participants have sufficient information to engage in activity, called arbitrage, that works to keep the market price of ETF shares closely linked to the ETF's underlying value.

A Word on *Active* and *Passive Investing*

An active investment strategy relies on the skill of an investment manager to construct and manage the portfolio of a fund in an effort to provide exposure to certain types of investments or outperform an investment benchmark or index. An actively managed fund has the potential to outperform the market, but its performance is dependent on the skill of the manager. Also, actively managed funds historically have had higher management fees, which can significantly lower investment returns. The shareholder is paying for more active management of portfolio assets, which often leads to higher turnover costs in the portfolio and potentially negative federal income tax consequences.

Passive investing is an investment strategy that is designed to achieve approximately the same return as a particular market index, before fees. The strategy can be implemented by replication—purchasing 100% of the securities in the same proportion as in the index or benchmark—or by a representative sampling of stocks in the index. Passive investing also typically comes with lower management fees. As discussed above, passively managed mutual funds are typically called index funds.

Most ETFs are also passively managed, although there are some actively managed ETFs on the market. Passively managed ETFs typically have lower costs for the same reasons index mutual funds do. In addition, index-based ETFs' costs and taxes can be even lower than index mutual funds' because of the manner in which ETFs operate.

■ **Leveraged, inverse and inverse leveraged ETFs**
Leveraged, inverse, and inverse leveraged ETFs seek to achieve a daily return that is a multiple or inverse multiple of the daily return of a securities index. These ETFs are a subset of index-based ETFs because they track a securities index. They seek to achieve their stated objectives on a daily basis. Investors should be aware that the performance of these ETFs over a period longer than one day will probably differ significantly from their stated daily performance objectives. These ETFs often employ techniques such as engaging in short sales and using swaps, futures contracts and other derivatives that can expose the ETF, and by extension the ETF investors, to a host of risks. *As such, these are specialized products that typically are not suitable for buy-and-hold investors.*

A Word about *Exchange-Traded Managed Funds (ETMF)*

An exchange-traded managed fund (ETMF) is a new kind of registered investment company that is a hybrid between traditional mutual funds and exchange-traded funds. Like ETFs, ETMFs list and trade on a national exchange, directly issue and redeem shares only in creation units, and primarily use in-kind transfers of the basket of portfolio securities in issuing and redeeming creation units. Like mutual funds, ETMFs are bought and sold at prices linked to NAV and disclose their portfolio holdings quarterly with a 60-day delay. This structure may allow the product to provide certain cost and tax efficiencies of ETFs while maintaining the confidentiality of the current holdings similar to mutual funds. By not having to disclose their holdings on a daily basis as ETFs do, ETMFs may have an advantage in trying to outperform their benchmarks over time because they are less susceptible to front running by other investors who would be able to trade on the holdings' disclosures.

How Mutual Funds and ETFs Can Provide Returns to Investors

Investors can make money from their investments in three ways:

1. **Dividend Payments**—Depending on the underlying securities, a mutual fund or ETF may earn income in the form of dividends on the securities in its portfolio. The mutual fund or ETF then pays its shareholders nearly all of the income (minus disclosed expenses) it has earned.

2. **Capital Gains Distributions**—The price of the securities a mutual fund or ETF owns may increase. When a mutual fund or ETF sells a security that has increased in price, the mutual fund or ETF has a capital gain. At the end of the year, most mutual funds and ETFs distribute these capital gains (minus any capital losses) to shareholders. ETFs seek to minimize these capital gains by making in-kind exchanges to redeeming Authorized Participants instead of selling portfolio securities.

3. **Increased NAV/Increased Market Price**—If the market value of a mutual fund's portfolio increases, after deduction of expenses and liabilities, then the net asset value of the mutual fund and its shares increases. If the market value of an ETF's portfolio increases, after deduction of expenses and liabilities, then the net asset value of the ETF increases, and the market price of its shares may also increase.

With respect to dividend payments and capital gains distributions, mutual funds usually will give investors a choice: the mutual fund can send the investor a check or other form of payment, or the investor can have the dividends or distributions reinvested in the mutual fund to buy more shares (often without paying an additional sales load). If an ETF investor wants to reinvest a dividend payment or capital gains distribution, the process can be more complicated and the investor may have to pay additional brokerage commissions. Investors should check with their ETF or investment professional.

Things That Could Reduce Mutual Funds' and ETFs' Returns

Investors should consider the effect that fees, expenses, and taxes will have on their returns over time. They can significantly reduce the returns on mutual funds and ETFs.

Fees and Expenses

As with any business, running a mutual fund or ETF involves costs. Funds pass along these costs to investors by imposing fees and expenses.

Shareholder fees are fees charged directly to mutual fund investors in connection with transactions such as buying, selling, or exchanging shares, or on a periodic basis with respect to account fees. An investor can find these fees and charges listed in the "Fee Table" section of a mutual fund's prospectus or summary prospectus under the heading, "Shareholder Fees." ETFs don't charge these fees directly to investors, but they may have several types of transaction fees and costs, which are described below.

Operating expenses are ongoing mutual fund and ETF costs such as investment advisory fees for managing the fund's holdings, marketing and distribution expenses, as well as custodial, transfer agency, legal, and accountant's fees. Operating expenses are regular and recurring fund-wide expenses that are typically paid out of fund assets, which means that investors indirectly pay these costs. These expenses are identified in the "Fee Table" section of a mutual fund's or ETF's prospectus or summary prospectus under the heading, "Annual Fund Operating Expenses." Although these fees and expenses may not be listed individually as specific line items on an account statement, they can have a substantial impact on an investment over time.

Fees and expenses vary from fund to fund. If the funds are otherwise the same, a fund with lower fees will outperform a fund with higher fees. Remember, the more investors pay in fees and expenses, the less money they will have in their investment portfolio. As noted above, index funds typically have lower fees than actively managed funds.

PROSPECTUS FEE TABLE

The following discussion details the disclosure required in the fee table in a mutual fund or ETF prospectus. ETFs don't charge shareholder fees (that are required to be included in the fee table) directly to investors. But, they may have several types of transaction fees and costs which are also described below.

Fee Table: Shareholder Fees for mutual funds (fees paid directly from an investment)

■ **Sales Charge (Load) on Purchases**—a fee some mutual funds charge investors when they buy shares, also known as a **front-end load**. This fee is typically paid to the broker that sells the mutual fund's shares. In this respect, a sales load is like a commission investors pay when they purchase any type of security (like a stock or an ETF) from a broker. Front-end loads reduce the amount of an investment. For example, let's say an investor has $1,000 and wants to invest it in a mutual fund with a 5% front-end load. The $50 sales load the investor must pay comes off the top of the investment leaving the remaining $950 to be invested in the mutual fund.

■ **Purchase Fee**—a fee some mutual funds charge investors when they buy shares. Unlike a front-end sales load, a purchase fee is paid into fund assets (not to a broker) and is typically imposed to defray some of the mutual fund's costs associated with the purchase. This fee is often imposed by a mutual fund that has high transaction costs, for example, because of its investment strategy. The fee is designed so that the other investors' investments in the mutual fund are not diminished by the transaction costs of the purchase. Like front-end sales loads, purchase fees reduce the amount of the investment.

■ **Deferred Sales Charge (Load)**—a fee some mutual funds charge investors when they sell or redeem their shares, also known as a **back-end load**. This fee is typically paid to the broker that sells the mutual fund's shares. The most common type of back-end sales load is the **contingent deferred sales load** (also known as the CDSC or CDSL). The amount of this type of sales load will depend on how long the investor holds his or her shares. It typically decreases to zero if the investor holds his or her shares for a specified time period. When an investor purchases shares that are subject to a back-end sales load rather than a front-end sales load, no sales load is deducted at purchase, and all of the investors' money is immediately used to purchase fund shares (assuming that no other fees or charges apply at the time of purchase). However, a back-end sales load will reduce an investor's return on the investment. Typically, a fund calculates the amount of a back-end sales load based on the lesser of the value of the investor's initial investment or the value of the investment at redemption.

■ **Redemption Fee**—a fee some mutual funds charge investors when they sell or redeem their shares within a certain time frame of purchasing the shares. Unlike a deferred sales load, a redemption fee is paid into fund assets (not to the broker) and is typically used to defray fund costs associated with an investor's redemption. The SEC limits redemption fees to 2%.

■ **Exchange Fee**—a fee some mutual funds charge investors when they exchange (transfer) their investment to another fund within the same fund group or family of funds.

■ **Account Fee**—a fee some mutual funds charge investors in connection with the maintenance of their accounts. For example, some funds impose an account maintenance fee on accounts whose value is less than a certain dollar amount.

Transaction fees and costs for ETFs not reflected in the Fee Table

■ **Brokerage Commissions**—ETF investors typically pay their brokers sales commissions with each purchase or sale of ETF shares, although some ETFs may be available commission-free. In this respect, a commission is like a sales load investors pay when purchasing or redeeming a mutual fund. Like front-end sales loads, brokerage commissions on a purchase reduce the amount of the investment. Like back-end sales loads, brokerage commissions on a sale reduce an investor's return on the investment. A brokerage commission may be structured as a flat fee charged every time an investor trades. With a flat fee, the smaller the amount traded, the larger the percentage cost per trade is. Investors should consider the fee structure of a commission when purchasing or selling ETF shares. Check with your broker regarding these fees. Brokers should provide written notice to customers of these charges when accounts are opened and when any of the charges change.

■ **Bid-ask spread**—ETFs and other securities that trade on a securities market actually have two market prices— the bid price and the ask price. The term bid refers to the highest price a buyer will pay to buy a specified number of ETF shares at any given time. The term ask refers to the lowest price at which a seller will sell the ETF shares. The bid price will be lower than the ask price and the difference between two prices is called the spread. An example is an ETF share that is trading for $59.50/$60. The bid price is $59.50, the ask price is $60.00, and the spread is 50 cents. If an investor buys 200 ETF shares at the ask price of $60 and sells them immediately at the bid price of $59.50, the investor would incur a loss of $100. This example demonstrates the impact of the spread on an ETF investment. ETFs that are more liquid and have higher trading volume have tighter or smaller spreads. The spread can be thought of as a hidden cost to investors since spreads reduce potential returns.

■ **Changes in discounts and premiums to NAV**—For a variety of reasons, an ETF's market price may reflect a premium or a discount to the ETF's underlying value or NAV. This is a potential cost but also a potential gain. An ETF share is trading at a premium when its market price is higher than the NAV or the value of its underlying holdings. An ETF share is trading at a discount when its market price is lower than the NAV or value of its underlying holdings. An investor may, therefore, pay more or less than the NAV when buying shares or receive more or less than NAV when selling shares.

A Word about *Exchanging Shares*

A family of funds is a group of mutual funds that share administrative and distribution systems. Each fund in a family may have different investment objectives and follow different strategies.

Some funds offer exchange privileges within a family of funds, allowing shareholders to directly transfer their holdings from one fund to another as their investment goals or tolerance for risk change. While some funds impose fees for exchanges, most funds typically do not. To learn more about a fund's exchange policies, call the fund's toll-free number, visit its website, or read the "Shareholder Information" section of the prospectus.

Bear in mind that exchanges have tax consequences. Even if the fund doesn't charge for the transfer, the investor will be liable for any capital gain on the sale of the old shares or, depending on the circumstances, eligible to take a capital loss (taxes are discussed generally on pages 39-40).

Fee Table: Annual Fund Operating Expenses (annual expenses paid as a percentage of the value of an investment)

■ **Management Fees**—fees paid out of mutual fund or ETF assets to the fund's investment adviser for investment portfolio management. They can also include any other management fees payable to the fund's investment adviser or its affiliates and administrative fees payable to the investment adviser that are not included in the Other Expenses category (discussed below).

■ **Distribution [and/or Service] (12b-1) Fees**—fees paid out of mutual fund or ETF assets to cover the costs of distribution (e.g., marketing and selling fund shares) and sometimes to cover the costs of providing shareholder services. **Distribution Fees** include fees to compensate brokers and others who sell fund shares and to pay for advertising, the printing and mailing of prospectuses to new investors, and the printing and mailing of sales literature. **Shareholder Service Fees** are fees paid to persons to respond to investor inquiries and provide investors with information about their investments. Shareholder service fees can be paid outside of 12b-1 fees, and if they are, they are included in the Other Expenses category (discussed below).

■ **Other Expenses**—fees paid out of mutual fund or ETF assets that are not already included under Management Fees or Distribution or Service (12b-1) Fees (such as any shareholder service expenses that are not already included in the 12b-1 fees), custodial expenses, legal and account expenses, transfer agent expenses and other administrative expenses.

■ **Total Annual Fund Operating Expenses (Expense Ratio)**—the line of the fee table that represents the total of a mutual fund's or ETF's annual fund operating expenses, expressed as a percentage of the fund's average net assets. Looking at the expense ratio can help investors make comparisons among various mutual funds and ETFs.

Investors should be sure to review carefully the fee tables of any mutual funds or ETFs they're considering, including no-load mutual funds. Even small differences in fees can translate into large differences in returns over time. For example, if an investor invested $10,000 in a fund that produced a 5% annual return before expenses and had annual operating expenses of 1.5%, then after 20 years the investor could have roughly $19,612. But if the fund had expenses of only 0.5%, then the investor would end up with $24,002—a 23% difference.

A Word about *No-Load Mutual Funds*

Some mutual funds call themselves *no-load*. As the name implies, this means that the mutual fund does not charge any type of sales load. But, as discussed above, not every type of shareholder fee is a sales load. A no-load fund may charge direct fees that are not sales loads, such as purchase fees, redemption fees, exchange fees, and account fees. No-load funds also will have annual fund operating expenses that investors pay for indirectly through fund assets.

Classes of Mutual Funds

Although ETFs offer only one class of shares, many mutual funds offer more than one class of shares. Each class will invest in the same portfolio of securities and will have the same investment objectives and policies. But each class will have different shareholder services and/or distribution arrangements with different fees and expenses. Because of the different fees and expenses, each class will likely have different performance results. A multi-class structure offers investors the ability to select a fee and expense structure that is most appropriate for their investment goals (including the time that they expect to remain invested in the fund). Here are some key characteristics of the most common mutual fund share classes offered to individual investors:

■ **Class A Shares**—Class A shares typically charge a front-end sales load, but they tend to have a lower 12b-1 fee and lower annual expenses than other mutual fund share classes. Some mutual funds reduce the front-end load as the size of the investment increases. These discounts are called breakpoints (discussed below).

■ **Class B Shares**—Class B shares typically do not have a front-end sales load. Instead, they may charge a contingent deferred sales load and a 12b-1 fee (along with other annual expenses). Typically the amount of the contingent deferred sales load decreases the longer an investor holds the shares. Class B shares also might convert automatically to a class with a lower 12b-1 fee and no contingent deferred sales load if the investor holds the shares long enough.

■ **Class C Shares**—Class C shares might have a 12b-1 fee, other annual expenses, and either a front-end or back-end sales load. But the front-end or back-end load for Class C shares tends to be lower than for Class A or Class B shares, respectively. Unlike Class B shares, Class C shares generally do not convert to another class; as a result, the back-end load will not decrease over time. Class C shares tend to have higher annual expenses than either Class A or Class B shares.

■ **Other Classes**—Other classes may also exist for some funds.

A Word about *Breakpoints*

Some mutual funds that charge front-end sales loads will charge lower sales loads for larger investments. In the prospectus fee table, they are referred to as sales charge discounts, but the investment levels required to obtain a reduced sales load are more commonly referred to as **breakpoints**.

The SEC does not require a mutual fund to offer breakpoints in its sales load. But, if the mutual fund offers breakpoints, the mutual fund must disclose them and brokers must apply them. In addition, a brokerage firm is not allowed to sell shares of a mutual fund in an amount that is just below the mutual fund's breakpoint simply to earn a higher commission.

Each fund company establishes its own formula for how it will calculate whether an investor is entitled to receive a breakpoint. For that reason, it is important for investors to seek out breakpoint information from their financial advisors or the mutual fund itself. An investor will need to ask how a particular mutual fund establishes eligibility for breakpoint discounts, as well as what the mutual fund's breakpoint amounts are. Some of this information is also included in the "Fee Table" section of the mutual fund's prospectus or summary prospectus.

Tax Consequences

When an investor buys and holds an individual stock or bond, the investor must pay income tax each year on the dividends or interest received. But the investor won't have to pay any capital gains tax until he or she actually sells and unless he or she makes a profit. Mutual funds and ETFs are somewhat different.

As with an individual stock, when an investor buys and holds mutual fund or ETF shares the investor will owe income tax each year on any dividends received. In addition, the investor will also owe taxes on any personal capital gains in years when an investor sells shares.

However, unlike with an individual stock, an investor may also have to pay taxes each year on the mutual fund's or ETF's capital gains even if the mutual fund or ETF has had a negative return and the investor hasn't sold any shares. That's because the law requires mutual funds and ETFs to distribute any net capital gains on the sale of portfolio securities to shareholders. ETFs are typically more tax efficient in this regard than mutual funds because ETF shares are frequently redeemed in-kind by the Authorized Participants. This means that an ETF may deliver specified portfolio securities to Authorized Participants who are redeeming creation units instead of selling portfolio securities to meet redemption demands. The selling of portfolio securities could otherwise result in taxable capital gains to the ETF that would typically be passed through to the retail investor. Nevertheless, the tax efficiency of ETFs is not relevant if an investor holds the mutual fund or ETF investment in a tax-advantaged account, such as an IRA or a 401(k).

SEC rules require mutual funds and ETFs to disclose in their prospectuses after-tax returns. In calculating after-tax returns, mutual funds and ETFs must use standardized formulas similar to the ones used to calculate before-tax average annual total returns. A fund's after-tax returns are discussed in the "Investments, Risks and Performance" section of the prospectus. When comparing mutual funds and/or ETFs, be sure to take taxes into account.

A Word about *Tax Exempt Funds*

If an investor invests in a tax-exempt fund—such as a municipal bond fund—some or all of the dividends will be exempt from federal (and sometimes state and local) income tax. The investor will, however, owe taxes on any capital gains.

Sources of Information

▦ Prospectus and Summary Prospectus

Mutual funds must provide a copy of the fund's prospectus to shareholders after they purchase shares, but investors can—and should—request and read the mutual fund's prospectus *before* making an investment decision. There are two kinds of prospectuses: (1) the statutory prospectus; and (2) the summary prospectus. The statutory prospectus is the traditional, long-form prospectus with which most mutual fund investors are familiar. The summary prospectus, which is used by many mutual funds, is just a few pages long and contains key information about a mutual fund. The SEC specifies the kinds of information that must be included in mutual fund prospectuses and requires mutual funds to present the information in a standard format so that investors can readily compare different mutual funds.

The same key information required in the summary prospectus is required to be in the beginning of the statutory prospectus. It appears in the following standardized order: (1) investment objectives/goals; (2) fee table; (3) investments, risks, and performance; (4) management—investment advisers and portfolio managers; (5) purchase and sale of fund shares; (6) tax information; and (7) financial intermediary compensation. Investors can also find more detailed information in the statutory prospectus, including financial highlights information.

An ETF will also have a prospectus, and some ETFs may have a summary prospectus, both of which are subject to the same legal requirements as mutual fund prospectuses and summary prospectuses. All investors who purchase creation units (i.e., Authorized Participants) receive a prospectus. Some broker-dealers also deliver a prospectus to secondary market purchasers. All ETFs are required to deliver a prospectus upon request and without charge, and the prospectus will usually be available on the ETF's website.

While they may seem daunting at first, mutual fund and ETF prospectuses contain valuable information. Here's some of what is included in mutual fund and ETF prospectuses:

- **Investment Objective**—The prospectus will describe the mutual fund's or ETF's investment objectives or goals. A fund may also identify its type or category (e.g., that it is a money market fund or balanced fund).

- **Fee Table**—This table describes the mutual fund's or ETF's fees and expenses, which include the shareholder fees and annual fund operating expenses (discussed on pages 29-36). The fee table includes an example that will help investors compare costs among different mutual funds or ETFs by showing them the costs associated with investing a hypothetical $10,000 over a 1-, 3-, 5-, and 10-year period.

- **Key Risks**—The prospectus will discuss the mutual fund's or ETF's principal investment risks.

- **Financial Highlights Information**—This section, which generally appears towards the back of the prospectus, contains audited data concerning the mutual fund's or ETF's financial performance for each of the past 5 years. Here an investor will find net asset values (for both the beginning and end of each period), total returns, and various ratios, including the ratio of expenses to average net assets, the ratio of net income to average net assets, and the portfolio turnover rate.

■ Statement of Additional Information (SAI)

The SAI explains a mutual fund's or ETF's operations in greater detail than the prospectus—including the mutual fund's or ETF's financial statements and details about the history of the mutual fund or ETF, its policies on borrowing and concentration, the identity of officers, directors and persons who control the mutual fund or ETF, investment advisory and other services, brokerage commissions paid on portfolio securities transactions, tax matters, and performance such as yield and average annual total return information. If an investor asks, the mutual fund or ETF must send an SAI. The back cover of the mutual fund's or ETF's prospectus should contain information on how to obtain the SAI.

■ Shareholder Reports

A mutual fund also must provide shareholders with annual and semi-annual reports within 60 days after the end of the fund's fiscal year and 60 days after the fund's fiscal mid-year. These reports contain updated financial information, a list of the fund's portfolio securities, and other information. The information in the shareholder reports will be current as of the date of the report (that is, the last day of the fund's fiscal year for the annual report, and the last day of the fund's fiscal mid-year for the semi-annual report). Investors can obtain all of these documents by:

- Visiting the mutual fund's or ETF's website;

- Calling or writing to the mutual fund or ETF (all mutual funds and ETFs have toll-free telephone numbers);

- Contacting a broker that sells the mutual fund's or ETF's shares;

- Searching the SEC's EDGAR database (www.sec.gov/edgar/searchedgar/mutualsearch.html) and downloading the documents for free; or

- Contacting the SEC's Office of Investor Education and Advocacy by telephone (800) 732-0330.

Avoiding Common Pitfalls

Past Performance

A mutual fund's or ETF's past performance is not as important as one might think. Advertisements, rankings, and ratings often emphasize how well a mutual fund or ETF has performed in the past. But studies show that the future is often different. This year's number one mutual fund or ETF can easily become next year's below average mutual fund or ETF.

For mutual funds and ETFs, be sure to find out how long the fund has been in existence. Newly created or small mutual funds or ETFs sometimes have excellent short-term performance records. Because newly created mutual funds and ETFs may invest in only a small number of stocks, a few successful stocks can have a large impact on their performance. But as these mutual funds and ETFs grow larger and increase the number of stocks they own, each stock has less impact on performance. This may make it more difficult to sustain initial results.

While past performance does not necessarily predict future returns, it *can* tell an investor how volatile (or stable) a mutual fund or ETF has been over a period of time. Generally, the more volatile a fund, the higher the investment risk. If you will need your money to meet a financial goal in the near-term, you probably can't afford the risk of investing in a fund with a volatile history because you will not have enough time to ride out any declines in the stock market.

For index mutual funds and index ETFs, remember that these funds are designed to track a particular market index and their past performance is related to how well that market index did.

Looking Beyond A Mutual Fund or ETF Name

Don't assume that a mutual fund called the "ZYX Stock Fund" invests *only* in stocks or that the "Martian High-Yield Fund" invests only in the securities of companies headquartered on the planet Mars. The SEC generally requires that any mutual fund or ETF with a name suggesting that it focuses on a particular type of investment must invest at least 80% of its assets in the type of investment suggested by its name. But mutual funds and ETFs can still invest up to one-fifth of their holdings in other types of securities—including securities that a particular investor might consider too risky or perhaps not aggressive enough.

Bank Products Versus Mutual Funds

Many banks now sell mutual funds, some of which carry the bank's name. But mutual funds sold in banks, including money market funds, are *not* bank deposits. As a result, they are *not* federally insured by the Federal Deposit Insurance Corporation (FDIC).

Money Market Matters

Don't confuse a money market fund with a money market deposit account. The names are similar, but they are completely different.

A money market fund is a type of mutual fund. It is not guaranteed or FDIC-insured. When an investor buys shares in a money market fund, he or she should receive a prospectus.

A money market deposit account is a bank deposit. It is guaranteed and FDIC-insured. When a saver deposits money in a money market deposit account, he or she should receive a Truth in Savings form.

If You Have a Question or Complaint

If you have a question or complaint about your mutual fund or ETF, you can send it to us using this online form (www.sec.gov/complaint/select.shtml). You can also reach us by regular mail, by telephone, or by fax at:

U.S. Securities and Exchange Commission
Office of Investor Education and Advocacy
100 F Street, N.E.
Washington, D.C. 20549-0213
Toll-free: (800) 732-0330
Fax: (202) 772-9295

For more information about investing wisely and avoiding fraud, please check out www.Investor.gov.

Glossary of Key Mutual Fund and ETF Terms

12b-1 Fees—fees paid out of mutual fund or ETF assets to cover the costs of marketing and selling mutual fund shares and sometimes to cover the costs of providing shareholder services. Distribution fees include fees to compensate brokers and others who sell fund shares and to pay for advertising, the printing and mailing of prospectuses to new investors, and the printing and mailing of sales literature. Shareholder Service Fees are fees paid to persons to respond to investor inquiries and provide investors with information about their investments.

Account Fee—a fee that some mutual funds separately charge investors for the maintenance of their accounts. For example, accounts below a specified dollar amount may have to pay an account fee.

Authorized Participants—financial institutions, which are typically large broker-dealers, who enter into contractual relationships with ETFs to buy and redeem creation units of ETF shares.

Back-end Load—a sales charge (also known as a deferred sales charge) investors pay when they redeem (or sell) mutual fund shares; generally used by the mutual fund to compensate brokers.

Brokers—an individual who acts as an intermediary between a buyer and seller, usually charging a commission to execute trades.

Brokerage Commissions—A fee investors pay their brokers with each purchase or sale of ETF shares.

Classes—different types of shares issued by a single mutual fund, often referred to as *Class A* shares, *Class B* shares, and so on. Each class invests in the same pool (or investment portfolio) of securities and has the same investment objectives and policies. But each class has different shareholder services and/or distribution arrangements with different fees and expenses and therefore different performance results.

Closed-End Fund—a type of investment company that does not continuously offer its shares for sale but instead sells a fixed number of shares at one time (in the initial public offering) which then typically trade on a secondary market, such as the New York Stock Exchange or the Nasdaq Stock Market—legally known as a closed-end investment company.

Contingent Deferred Sales Load—a type of back-end load, the amount of which depends on the length of time the investor held his or her mutual fund shares. For example, a contingent deferred sales load might be (X)% if an investor holds his or her shares for one year, (X-1)%

after two years, and so on until the load reaches zero and goes away completely.

Conversion—a feature some mutual funds offer that allows investors to automatically change from one class to another (typically with lower annual expenses) after a set period of time. The mutual fund's prospectus or summary prospectus will state whether a class ever converts to another class.

Creation Units—large blocks of shares of an ETF, typically 50,000 shares or more, usually sold in in-kind exchanges to Authorized Participants.

Deferred Sales Charge—see back-end load (above).

Discount to NAV—when an ETF's market price is trading lower than the value of the underlying holdings.

Distribution Fees—fees paid out of mutual fund or ETF assets to cover expenses for marketing and selling mutual fund or ETF shares, including advertising costs, compensation for brokers and others who sell mutual fund shares, and payments for printing and mailing prospectuses to new investors and sales literature prospective investors—sometimes referred to as 12b-1 fees.

Exchange Fee—a fee that some mutual funds charge shareholders if they exchange (transfer) to another mutual fund within the same fund group.

Exchange-Traded Funds—a type of an investment company (either an open-end company or UIT) that differs from traditional mutual funds, because shares issued by ETFs trade on a secondary market and are only redeemable by Authorized Participants from the fund itself in very large blocks (blocks of 50,000 shares for example) called creation units.

Expense Ratio—a mutual fund's or ETF's total annual operating expenses (including management fees, distribution (12b-1) fees, and other expenses) expressed as a percentage of average net assets.

Front-end Load—an upfront sales charge investors pay when they purchase mutual fund shares, generally used by the mutual fund to compensate brokers. A front-end load reduces the amount available to purchase fund shares.

Index Fund or ETF—describes a type of mutual fund or ETF whose investment objective typically is to achieve the same return as a particular market index, such as the S&P 500 Composite Stock Price Index, the Russell 2000 Index, or the Wilshire 5000 Total Market Index.

Investment Adviser—generally, a person or entity who receives compensation for giving individually tailored advice to a specific person on investing in stocks, bonds, or mutual funds. Some investment advisers also manage portfolios of securities, including mutual funds.

Investment Company—a company (corporation, business trust, partnership, or limited liability company) that issues securities and is primarily engaged in the business of investing in securities. The three basic types of investment companies are open-end funds (mutual funds and most ETFs), closed-end funds, and unit investment trusts (some ETFs).

Load—see Sales Charge.

Management Fee—fee paid out of mutual fund or ETF assets to the fund's investment adviser or its affiliates for managing the fund's portfolio, any other management fee payable to the fund's investment adviser or its affiliates, and any administrative fee payable to the investment adviser that are not included in the "Other Expenses" category. A fund's management fee appears as a category under "Annual Fund Operating Expenses" in the Fee Table.

Market Index—a measurement of the performance of a specific basket of stocks or bonds considered to represent a particular market or sector of the U.S. stock market or the economy. For example, the Dow Jones Industrial Average (DJIA) is an index of 30 blue chip U.S. stocks of industrial companies (excluding transportation and utility companies).

Mutual Fund—the common name for an open-end investment company. Like other types of investment companies, mutual funds pool money from many investors and invest the money in stocks, bonds, short-term money-market instruments, or other securities. Mutual funds issue redeemable shares that investors purchase directly from the fund (or through a broker for the fund) instead of purchasing from investors on a secondary market.

NAV (Net Asset Value)—the per-share value of the mutual fund's or ETF's assets minus its liabilities. SEC rules require mutual funds and ETFs to calculate the NAV at least once daily. To calculate the NAV per share, a fund subtracts the fund's liabilities from its assets and then divides the result by the number of shares outstanding.

No-load Fund—a mutual fund that does not charge any type of sales load. But not every type of shareholder fee is a sales load, and a no-load fund may charge fees that are not sales loads. No-load funds also charge operating expenses.

Open-End Company—the legal name for a mutual fund and most ETFs. An open-end company is a type of investment company.

Operating Expenses—the costs a mutual fund or ETF incurs in connection with running the fund, including management fees, distribution (12b-1) fees, and other expenses.

Portfolio—an individual's or entity's combined holdings of stocks, bonds, or other securities and assets.

Premium to NAV—when an ETF's market price is trading higher than the value of the underlying holdings.

Prospectus—disclosure document that describes the mutual fund or ETF. Each mutual fund or ETF has a prospectus. The prospectus contains information about the fund's costs, investment objectives, risks, and performance. You can get a prospectus from the mutual fund company or ETF sponsor (through its website or by phone or mail). Your financial professional or broker can also provide you with a copy.

Purchase Fee—a shareholder fee that some mutual funds charge when investors purchase mutual fund shares. Not the same as (and may be in addition to) a front-end load.

Redemption Fee—a shareholder fee that some mutual funds charge when investors redeem (or sell) mutual fund shares within a certain time frame of purchasing the shares. Redemption fees (which must be paid to the fund) are not the same as (and may be in addition to) a back-end load (which is typically paid to a broker). The SEC generally limits redemption fees to 2%.

Sales Charge (or Load)—the amount that investors pay when they purchase (front-end load) or redeem (back-end load) shares in a mutual fund, similar to a brokerage commission.

Secondary Market—markets where existing securities are bought and sold.

Shareholder Fees—fees charged directly to investors in connection with particular investor transactions such as buying, selling, or exchanging shares or periodically with respect to account fees including sales loads, purchase or redemption fees.

Shareholder Service Fees—fees paid out of mutual fund or ETF assets to persons to respond to investor inquiries and provide investors with information about their investments. See also 12b-1 fees.

Statement of Additional Information (SAI)—disclosure document that provides information about a mutual fund or ETF in addition to, and sometimes in more detail, than the prospectus. Although mutual funds and ETFs are not required to provide investors with the SAI, they must give investors the SAI upon request and without charge.

Summary Prospectus—a disclosure document that summarizes key information for mutual funds and ETFs.

Total Annual Fund Operating Expense—the total of a mutual fund's or ETF's annual fund operating expenses, expressed as a percentage of the fund's average net assets. The total annual fund operating expenses is included in the fund's fee table in the prospectus.

Unit Investment Trust (UIT)—a type of investment company that typically makes a one-time public offering of only a specific, fixed number of units. A UIT will terminate and dissolve on a date established when the UIT is created (although some may terminate more than fifty years after they are created). UITs do not actively trade their investment portfolios.

SEC

OFFICE *of* INVESTOR
EDUCATION *and* ADVOCACY

Before You Invest,
Investor.gov

SEC Pub. 182 (12/16)